Dictionary of Phrasal Verbs

Dictionary of Phrasal Verbs

Najmussehar

PRABHAT
PAPERBACKS

Published by
PRABHAT PAPERBACKS
An imprint of Prabhat Prakashan Pvt. Ltd.
4/19 Asaf Ali Road,
New Delhi-110 002 (INDIA)
e-mail: prabhatbooks@gmail.com

ISBN 978-93-5186-009-9
Dictionary of Phrasal Verbs
by Najmussehar

Edition
2023

Price
₹ 250.00 (Rupees Two Hundred Fifty only)

Printed at
Narula Printers, Delhi

PHRASAL VERBS

Phrasal verbs are part of a large group of verbs called "multi-word verbs". Phrasal verbs and other multi-word verbs are an important part of the English language. Multi-word verbs, including phrasal verbs, are very common, especially in spoken English. A multi-word verb is a combination of two or more words, like "pick up", "turn on" or "get on with". For convenience, many people refer to all multi-word verbs as phrasal verbs. These verbs consist of a basic verb + another word or words. The other word(s) can be prepositions and/or adverbs. The two or three words that make up multi-word verbs form a short "phrase", which is why these verbs are often called "phrasal verbs".

The important thing to remember is that a multi-word verb is still a verb. "Get" is a verb. "Get up", is also a verb, a different verb. "Get" and "get up" are two different verbs. They do not have the same meaning. So you should treat each multi-word verb as a separate verb, and learn it like any other verb.

English phrasal verbs come in many shapes and sizes.

Typically, they're a combination of verb and preposition which, when combined, changes the meaning of the main verb.

Most students of English find them difficult because sometimes the idiomatic uses either make no sense at all, or the change in meaning is so drastic that even a good guesser has no idea what they mean.

Sometimes we call them two-part verbs, three-part verbs, or multi-word verbs.

Whatever you call them, you should know some basic truths regarding phrasal verb usage.

First of all, they are often used in a literal sense. That is, the combination of the verb with the preposition leads to a logical understanding. There are times when the meaning is far removed from the original verb and takes on a completely idiomatic usage.

Example: The boy jumped on the bed.

Jumped on literally means what it says.

Example: The boy in the race jumped into the lead.

Jumped into (almost literally) means what it says. This is bordering on idiomatic, but it is still somewhat literal.

Idiomatic Usage

The problems begin when the verb "jump" is combined with other prepositions or adverbs that give it a completely idiomatic meaning.

Example: "Did you get the weekend off?"

"Yes, but I had to jump through all the hoops."

Here, "jump through" has a metaphorical, or idiomatic meaning. It means, "forced or made to do something unpleasant; made to follow procedure". (Think of a lion or tiger performing at the circus...being made, or forced by the whip, to jump through the hoops the lion tamer is holding.)

The above is quite typical when it comes to phrasal verb usage. The good thing is that these verbs often follow set patterns.

Phrasal Verb Patterns

Phrasal verbs can be either intransitive or transitive. That is, they are either followed by an object, or not. An intransitive verb does not have an object while a transitive verb does.

Difficulties sometimes occur when deciding if a verb can be "separated" from the preposition that forms the phrasal verb. The following examples illustrate the problem.

Example: Turn off the TV.

Example: Turn the TV off.

As seen above, some phrasal verbs can be separated with the object of the verb coming between the main verb and the preposition. It's important to know and remember, however, that some phrasal verbs cannot be separated, and the verb and preposition must remain together.

Example: The sewer gave off a horrible smell.

NOT: The sewer gave a horrible smell off.

Some verbs require that the object comes before the adverb.

Example: They allowed the boy through.

NOT: They allowed through the boy.

When dealing with transitive verbs and the object is a pronoun, then the pronoun comes before the adverb.

Example: Turn it on.

NOT: Turn on it.

CONTENTS

A

Abide by	– adhere to; respect or obey (the law, a decision, a rule)
Account for	– explain; give a reason
Ache for	– want something or someone a lot
Act on	– to take action because of something, like information received
Act out	– perform something with actions and gestures; express an emotion in your behaviour
Act up	– behave badly or strangely; misbehave (for people); not work properly (for machines)
Add on	– include in a calculation
Add up	– make sense; find the total, logically fit together; seem reasonable; something equal; to total
Add up to	– have a certain result
Advise against	– recommend not doing something
Agree with	– have the same opinion as somebody else
Aim at	– point something in the direction of a target; to target

Allow for	– include something in a plan or calculation; take into consideration; include in a calculation; try to get something indirectly, by hinting or suggesting
Answer back	– to reply rudely to someone in authority, reply rudely
Answer for	– be held responsible for a problem; speak on behalf of someone or from knowing them
Appeal to	– plead or make an earnest request; be attractive or interesting
Apply for	– make a formal request for something (job, permit, loan, etc.)
Argue out	– argue about a problem to find a solution
Ask after	– enquire about someone's health, how life is going
Ask around	– ask a number of people for information or help; invite someone; ask many people the same question
Ask for	– request; to provoke a negative reaction; request to have or be given
Ask in	– to invite somebody into your house
Ask out	– to invite someone for a date; to ask someone to go on a date
Ask over	– invite
Ask round	– invite someone
Ask someone out	– invite on a date
Avail (oneself) of	– take advantage of something (an opportunity)

□

B

Back away	– move backwards, in fear or dislike; retreat or go backwards
Back down	– retract or withdraw your position or proposal in an argument
Back off	– not follow a threat; retreat
Back out	– fail to keep an arrangement or promise
Back out of	– fail to keep an agreement, arrangement
Back someone up	– support
Back something up	– reverse
Back up	– give support or encouragement; to move backwards; to make a copy of something in case the original is destroyed or lost; confirm a story, facts, or information; drive a vehicle backwards (in reverse) to make a "protection" copy to use if there are problems with the original, move in reverse
Bag out	– criticise; pay money to secure someone's release; rescue from financial difficulties

Bail out	– save; rescue; remove water from something that is flooded; jump out of a plane because it is going to crash
Bail out on	– stop supporting someone when they are in trouble
Bail up	– talk to someone and delay them; rob someone at gunpoint
Ball up	– confuse or make things complicated; roll or form into a round shape
Balls up	– spoil; ruin
Bang about/ Bang around	– move in a place making a lot of noise
Bang on about	– keep talking about something
Bang out	– play a musical instrument loudly
Bang up	– put someone in prison; damage badly
Bank on	– base your hopes on someone/ something; count or rely on; depend on
Bargain for	– take into account
Barge in/Barge into	– enter a place and interrupt people rudely
Bash about	– mistreat physically
Bash in/Bash up	– break; damage or injure/hurt by hitting
Bash out	– write something quickly without much preparation
Bawl out	– scold; shout at someone; sing or shout unpleasantly loudly
Be after	– try to find or get
Be along	– arrive
Be away	– be elsewhere; on holiday, etc.
Be cut out for	– be suitable; have the necessary qualities

Be cut up	– be upset
Be down	– be depressed; be reduced or less
Be down with	– be ill
Be fed up	– be bored, upset or sick of something
Be in	– be at home or at work; be submitted; arrive
Be in on	– be involved in
Be not on	– be unacceptable
Be off	– to be cancelled; to have gone bad
Be on	– be functioning (of machines); take place; take medication or drugs, especially when they affect the person badly
Be on about	– mean; try to say
Be onto	– pursue; be aware of someone's true nature
Be out	– be absent from a place
Be out of	– have no more left
Be out to	– attempt
Be over	– to be finished
Be snowed under	– have too much work
Be taken aback	– be shocked or surprised
Be taken with	– like something
Be up	– be out of bed; have increased or risen, when the time for something finishes or expires
Be up to	– be good enough; doing something naughty or wrong
Bear down on	– move towards
Bear on	– influence; affect
Bear out	– confirm that something is correct
Bear up	– resist pressure
Bear up under	– cope with something difficult or stressful
Bear with	– be patient; be patient with

Beat down – strong sunshine

Beat up – attack violently; to hurt someone badly by hitting and punching

Beaver away – work hard

Beaver away at – work hard doing something

Bed down – sleep somewhere less comfortable than normal; become established or successful over time

Bed out – move a plant outside

Beef up – improve; make more substantial; complain, make something stronger or more solid

Belt out – sing something loudly

Belt up – be quiet; fasten your seatbelt

Bend down – lower the top half of your body

Bend over – lower the top part of your body

Bend over backwards – do a lot to try to help or please someone

Black out – faint; lose consciousness; fall unconscious; lose light; censor text so that words cannot be read; have a temporary memory failure

Blare out – a loud sound or music

Blast off – leave the ground; spaceship or rocket

Blaze away – fire a gun repeatedly

Bliss out – be extremely relaxed and happy

Block in – park a car and obstruct another car; shade or fill in

Block off – obstruct an exit to prevent people from leaving; to separate using a barrier

Block out – stop light from entering or leaving; try not to think about or feel something because it is upsetting or painful

Block up – fill a space so that nothing can pass

Blow away – kill; beat rivals or competitors by a large margin; impress greatly, when the wind moves something from a place

Blow down – when the wind forces something to fall

Blow off – not keep an appointment; ignore; not do something

Blow out – extinguish candles, matches, etc.

Blow over – when a scandal gets forgotten

Blow something up – add air

Blow up – to explode; be destroyed by an explosion; to fill a balloon/a tyre/ a football/etc. with air; to inflate; suddenly become very angry

Blurt out – to say something quickly without thinking, especially when you shouldn't

Bog down – to make slow progress

Bog in/Bog into – to eat something enthusiastically

Bog off – get lost

Boil down – to simplify; to reduce to the essentials

Boil down to – amount to; be summarized as

Boil over – when a hot liquid spills out of a container, when people lose their tempers and things get nasty

Boil up – feel a negative emotion strongly; cook or heat something to boiling point

Bone up on – review/study thoroughly for a short time, study hard

Book in/Book into – make a reservation in advance; check in at a hotel

Book up – to reserve

Boot up – to start a computer; to start a computer by loading an operating system or program

Border on – be located next to a place; be very nearly something; be near; be next to

Boss about/Boss around – use excessive authority to control people

Botch up – ruin or spoil something

Bottle away – store up

Bottle out – lack courage to do something

Bottle up – not express your feelings

Bottom out – pass the lowest point and start rising

Bounce back – recover

Bounce into – force someone

Bounce off – test ideas

Bowl over – surprise someone greatly

Box in – prevent something from moving, especially vehicles

Box up – pack things in boxes to move them

Branch out – move into a different area of business, etc.

Break into – to enter somewhere (e.g. a house) illegally, especially by force

Break off – break a piece from something; end a relationship; discontinue (therapy, relationship)

Break off talks – to end; to interrupt; to discontinue; stop talking

Break something down – divide into smaller parts

Breakaway – escape from captivity, leave an organisation, usually to form a new one

Breakdown – end negotiations unsuccessfully; start crying; stop working, go out of order; cease to function; lose control of one's emotions; fail to function; have a physical or mental collapse; get upset; stop functioning (vehicle, machine); separate something into component parts; to lose control emotionally or mentally

Break-in – force entry to a building; enter by using force (and breaking a lock, window, etc.); interrupt a discussion, burgle; soften with use (shoes); get someone/something accustomed to a new routine; wear something new until it's/they're comfortable

Breakout – to start suddenly; to escape from prison; begin suddenly

Breakout in something – develop a skin condition

Breakout in spots – to become covered by (something)

Breakout of – escape

Breakthrough – pass a barrier or obstacle

Break-up – break into many pieces; close an educational institution for the holidays; finish a relationship; become inaudible over the telephone because of interference

Breeze along – move easily and quickly

Breeze in/Breeze into – enter a place quickly

Breeze through – pass easily; succeed

Brighten up – to improve (weather); become happier; to make something more attractive or pleasant

Bring – return something

Bring about – to cause to happen; make something happen

Bring along – to bring someone or something to certain place; help someone improve

Bring around – persuade or convince someone; bring something with you when you visit; get someone talking about something

Bring back – cause someone to remember; return

Bring down – to make a Government fall; make something cheaper; make unhappy

Bring forth – produce something; make it known or visible; make something happen; remove something from where it is kept or hidden; give birth to

Bring forward – make something happen earlier than originally planned; draw attention to

Bring in – earn

Bring off – accomplish something difficult; succeed in doing something

Bring on – cause the onset of an illness; cause trouble to happen to oneself; cause to happen or appear, cause something to happen or speed up the process

Bring out – release or publish

Bring out in – cause a health problem or reaction

Bring round – make someone wake up from unconsciousness or an anaesthetic, (influence someone to your point of view); persuade

Bring up – to raise a child; start talking about a subject; vomit; mention as a topic of discussion; to take care of a child until it is fully grown and able to care for itself; to train and prepare a child for adult life

Brush off – ignore; pay little attention

Brush up – improve a skill quickly

Brush up on – improve; refresh one's knowledge of something; to review/study thoroughly for a short time

Bubble over – to become very excited

Bucket down – to rain heavily

Budge up – to move to make space for someone

Buff up – to clear, clean or make something shine; improve

Buff up on – to improve your knowledge quickly

Bug off – go away

Bug out – open your eyes wide in surprise; leave somewhere in a hurry

Build on – to develop from

Build up – develop a company; increase

Bulk out – to make something bigger or thicker

Bump into – to meet by accident or unexpectedly

Bump off – to kill

Bump up – to increase

Bundle off – to send someone somewhere

Bundle out – to expel

Bundle up – put on warm clothing; wrap or tie things together

Bunk off – absent from school, without permission

Buoy up – make someone feel more positive

Burn down – become destroyed/consumed by fire (Note: For upright things—trees, buildings, etc. only), to destroy by burning, burn completely

Burn off – to remove by burning or similar process

Burn out – lose enthusiasm and energy to continue in a demanding job; stop (something) working; become exhausted from over-working

Burn up – become destroyed/consumed by fire (Note: For people and non-upright things only); cause someone to become very angry

Burst into – catch fire very quickly; laugh; cry or clap loudly; suddenly enter

Butt in – impolitely interrupt (a conversation, an action); interrupt

Butt out – not be involved in other people's business

Butter up – praise or flatter someone excessively with the hope of getting some benefit

Buy in – force a CD or record into the charts by buying lots of copies

Buy into – accept an idea

Buy off – pay someone to stop them causing trouble

Buy out – buy somebody's share in a company

Buy up – buy all of something

Buzz around – move quickly around a place

Buzz off – go away; have an air of excitement

☐

C

Call after – name someone after somebody else

Call around – visit; phone many different places/people

Call back – return a phone call

Call for – demand; go to collect something; telephone for something; go and collect someone to take them out; require

Call forth – make something happen

Call in – get someone to come and do a job; stop and visit; communicate by phone; consult a specialist

Call off – cancel; order someone to stop attacking; cancel something that has been scheduled; to abandon something that has already begun

Call on – ask for help; visit; challenge; ask someone to do something; especially to speak in public; ask someone for an answer in class visit; ask to recite in class; ask, order, request somebody to do something

Call on someone – ask for an answer or opinion; visit someone

Call on/upon somebody – formally invite or request

Call out – read names aloud; order workers to strike

Call round – visit

Call up – summon someone for military service; to give a telephone call; mobilise for military service

Calm down – become more relaxed, less angry or upset; become less agitated; relax after being angry; stop being angry or emotionally excited

Cancel out – have an opposite effect on something that has happened; taking things back to the beginning

Care for – like; want (Note: This phrasal verb is usually negative, though it may be used affirmatively in questions), take care of, supply care to, attend/watch

Carry away – lose (a part of a ship) through breakage

Carry forward – include a figure in a later calculation, make something progress

Carry off – win; succeed; die of a disease; complete successfully despite a problem; take away (by force); win; remove; degrade (earth)

Carry on – continue, behave in a specified way

Carry on with – have an affair

Carry out – perform a task; food bought from a restaurant to take away; do something as specified (a plan, an order, a threat); perform or conduct (test, experiment); accomplish; make; complete a plan to fulfil or perform (something)

Carry over – continue past a certain point; postpone until later

Carry through – complete successfully; bring out of difficulties

Cart off – to take something or someone somewhere especially using a lot of effort

Cash in – convert shares, bonds, casino chips, etc. into money; obtain cash for

Cash in on – benefit or make money on something, especially if done unfairly

Cash out – illegally access a bank account or credit card and steal money

Cash up – count all the money taken in a shop or business at the end of the day

Catch at – take or grab hold of something

Catch on – become popular; develop understanding or knowledge of something; become popular; finally understand what is going on

Catch out – trick; discover or prove that someone is lying; put someone in an unexpected and difficult situation (often passive)

Catch up – get work, etc.; up to date; reach someone who was ahead of you

Catch up on – do something that should have been done earlier; reminisce with an old friend after not seeing him/her for a while

Catch up with – exchange news with (someone whom one has not seen for sometime); begin to have a damaging effect on

Cater for – to provide what is necessary

Cater to – to provide what is needed, often seen negatively

Cave in – collapse; stop resisting or refusing

Chalk out – to cut a line of cocaine

Chalk up – to achieve something good

Chalk up to – explain the reason for a problem

Chance upon – find something by accident

Change over – change a system, switch over

Change up – upgrade

Charge up – put electricity into a battery

Charge with – accuse somebody of a crime

Chase down – try hard to find or get something

Chase off – force a person to leave or go away

Chase up – ensure that someone remembers to do something, try to get someone to pay a bill, debt, etc.; try to get more information about the progress of something

Chat up – talk to someone you are sexually interested in to get them interested in you

Cheat on – be sexually unfaithful; deceive or betray, often in a sexual and/or emotional context

Cheat out of – get money from someone under false pretences

Check by – visit a place to check something

Check in – register at a hotel or airport; to report one's arrival; register for/at a hotel, conference, etc.; let someone know officially that you have arrived

Check into – register on arriving at a hotel or at the airport

Check off – make a mark to indicate that something on a list has been completed; mark something on a list as done

Check out – pay one's bill and leave (a hotel); to investigate; to follow procedures for borrowing something (usually for a limited period of time); leave a hotel; die; to stop paying attention to someone/something; look at (informal)

Check out of – settle up and pay before leaving a hotel

Check over – check something very carefully

Check up on – to examine/investigate; to track

Check with – to consult

Cheer on – to encourage

Cheer up – to become happier; help someone feel less worried/depressed/sad

Chew on – to consider; to scold someone severely; to berate; to think about something carefully before deciding

Chew out – criticise someone angrily

Chew over – think about an issue

Chew up – cut into small pieces with your teeth; damage something inside a machine

Chicken out – be too afraid to do something; lose the courage or confidence to do something often at the last minute

Chill out – relax

Chime in – contribute to a discussion

Chip away at – gradually reduce something to make it less powerful, effective, etc.

Chip in – contribute some money; contribute to a discussion; help; contribute/donate (often money) to something done by a group

Choose up – form groups or teams

Chop down – fell or cut down a tree

Chop up – cut into small pieces

Chuck away/Chuck out – dispose of something you no longer need or want

Chuck in – quit something; make a comment

Chuck up – vomit; be sick; quit something

Churn out – produce, usually quickly or in large amounts without much regard to quality

Clag up – make something sticky

Clam up – be quiet; refuse to speak; suddenly become quiet/refuse to talk about something

Clamp down on – act strictly to prevent something

Claw back – get money back; retake possession with difficulty

Clean out – tidy up thoroughly and throw away unwanted things; cause someone to spend all their money

Clean something up – to make tidy, clean

Clean up – tidy and clean
Clear away – leave a place; remove or tidy
Clear off – leave somewhere quickly
Clear up – cure or recover from an infection; tidy up; explain; improve (weather)
Click through – open an advertisement on the Internet
Climb down – accept that you are wrong and change your position
Clog up – block; slow movement right down
Close down – close a shop, branch or business permanently; stop an opponent being a challenge; stop operating (company, restaurant, cinema)
Close in – surround; envelop; approach; get near
Close in on/Close in upon – get near someone
Close off – block a place to stop people entering
Close on – get nearer
Close out – bring something to an end; close or stop using; ignore; exclude
Close up – completely close something; join together; move closer together
Cloud over – get very cloudy
Clown about/Clown around – behave stupidly or waste time
Cock up – ruin or spoil something
Colour (Color) up – blush
Come about – happen; occur; to be achieved
Come across – find by chance; appear; seem; make an impression; find something accidentally; find unexpectedly

Come after – follow
Come apart – break into pieces; separate
Come at – attack; reach; discover
Come back – return
Come before – appear in court charged with a crime or offence
Come by – pass; go past; visit; buy; get; acquire
Come down – rain; travel; fall (price)
Come down on – criticise heavily
Come down to – be in the end of a matter, mean, signify
Come down with – fall sick with
Come forth – appear
Come forth with – provide information
Come forward – volunteer for a task or to give evidence; present oneself
Come from – country or town where you were born, originate in
Come in – arrive for flights; place or ranking in a competition, etc.; receive news
Come in for – receive (criticism or praise), especially criticism, blame
Come into – be important or relevant; inherit; to receive something (usually money or property) after someone's death
Come into use – start being used
Come off – when something breaks off; be successful; to appear or seem to another person; become detached; take place successfully
Come off it – used to disagree with someone rudely, used as an imperative
Come on – encouragement; start an illness; start functioning (machines, etc.)

Come out	– a secret is revealed, be published or otherwise available to the public; disappear when washed; let people know that you are lesbian or gay; when the sun appears
Come out in	– have a rash or similar skin problem
Come out with	– make something available; say something publicly and unexpectedly
Come over	– feel strange; affect mentally in such a way as to change behaviour; come from a distance; to visit
Come round	– become conscious; wake up from anaesthesia; change your opinion
Come through	– arrive (messages and information); communicate an emotion; produce a result; succeed
Come through with	– provide something needed
Come to	– become conscious; wake up from anaesthesia; result in; total; amount to; arrive/reach a place; come to regain consciousness
Come up	– be mentioned/discussed, (problem); arise; draw near
Come up against	– be faced with (problems); meet a difficulty, be faced with or opposed by
Come up with	– think of a solution, excuse, etc.
Come upon	– discover; find/meet by chance
Confide in	– share a secret
Conjure up	– create a picture or memory in someone's mind; create

something without many resources

Conk out – breakdown suddenly or stop working; stop or fall asleep (from exhaustion)

Contract in – become involved or committed to something

Contract out – give a contract for a service outside the company you work for

Contract out of – formally leave an agreement

Cool down – get cooler; become calm

Coop up – confine in a small area

Cop it – get into trouble

Cop off – leave work or school early; kiss pet or have sex with someone

Cop out – choose an easy alternative

Cotton on – to work out the truth

Could do with – need or want something

Count in – include or involve

Count on – depend on; rely on; trust that something will happen or that someone will do as expected

Count out – exclude

Count up – add

Cozy up – make yourself comfortable

Cozy up to – make yourself popular with someone

Crack down on – use more authority than usual

Crack on – continue doing something with energy

Crack up – have a nervous breakdown; have bad reception on a mobile phone; burst out laughing; damage a car badly

Crank out – produce a lot of something fast

Crank up – inject non-medical drugs, start a machine, originally with a handle, increase, make something bigger

Crash out – sleep at someone's house because you are too tired, drunk, etc. to leave; fall asleep

Creep in – start to be noticeable; get included despite attempts to keep it or them out

Creep into – become noticeable in something

Creep out – make someone feel worried or uneasy

Creep out on – to do the same activity for a very long time

Creep over – start to have a negative feeling

Creep up on – approach without someone realising

Crop up – appear unexpectedly; happen unexpectedly

Cross off – delete; remove from a list

Cross out – put as line through some writing to show it is wrong; remove by drawing a line through

Crumb down – clear a table in a restaurant

Cry off – to cancel an arrangement

Cry out – shout because you are in pain

Cut across – go across a place rather than around it to make the journey quicker; affect people of different groups, classes, etc.; use a short route

Cut back/Cut back on – reduce expenditure; consume less, use less of something; to reduce in size or amount

Cut down – consume less; shoot; reduce a vertical thing to ground level by cutting; cut something from a high position

Cut in – start functioning; drive in front of another vehicle without warning; interrupt; include someone in a deal that makes money; mix fat and flour until they combine; start operating (of an engine or electrical device)

Cut it out – stop your unfair or unreasonable behaviour

Cut off – this verb can refer to either: (a) the service or supply that is cut off, e.g. water, electricity, etc. or (b) the person who is cut off to disconnect; interrupt or discontinue something or someone, remove with something sharp; stop providing; take out of a will; isolate or make inaccessible

Cut out – remove part of something (usually with scissors and paper); stop doing something, exclude, when an engine or motor stops; cut a picture or similar from a magazine, etc.

Cut out on – let down; snub; cut into smaller pieces; drive into a neighbouring lane, directly in front of another vehicle; upset; have a lot of small injuries

☐

D

Dash off	– leave somewhere quickly; do something quickly, especially writing
Dawn on	– finally realise or understand something; realize
Deal in	– stock, sell
Deal with	– handle; take care of (problem, situation)
Decide on	– settle on
Dial in	– calibrate
Die away	– become quieter or inaudible (of a sound)
Die down	– calm down; become less strong; decrease or become quieter
Die for	– want something a lot
Die off	– become extinct
Die out	– become extinct or disappear; to disappear completely
Dig in	– start eating greedily
Dig into	– reach inside to get something
Dig up	– find something that is supposed to be secret
Dine out	– have dinner outside your home
Dine out on	– tell a story repeatedly that is well received

Dip in	– put something in a liquid for a short time
Dip into	– read parts of a book, but not all; take money out of your savings
Dip out	– leave a place without telling anyone
Disagree with	– make someone feel sick or ill
Dish out	– serve food; give something, usually when you shouldn't; criticise, when you can't take criticism in return
Dish up	– serve food onto plates for a meal
Dispense with	– proceed without
Dispose of	– get rid of
Dive in	– start doing something, usually without planning; start eating
Dive into	– reach inside something quickly
Divvy out/Divvy up	– give out as ones share
Do away	– abolish; colloquial; murder; kill
Do away with	– abolish; get rid of
Do in	– to kill; to murder; cause to become very tired
Do out of	– cheat somebody out of something that is rightfully theirs
Do over	– do something again; repeat a job; beat up; do again
Do up	– close or fasten clothes, etc.; repair and renovate; to fasten; to button; to zip; to tie; to dress up; to repair; to improve the condition and appearance of something
Do with	– need
Do without	– manage without something; not require
Doss around/Doss about	– spend time doing very little or being unproductive

Doss down	– sleep somewhere temporarily because you don't go home
Doze off	– to fall asleep, usually accidentally
Drag on	– be unnecessarily long, last much longer than expected or is necessary
Draw back	– retreat; move backwards
Draw down	– reduce levels; get funding; to deplete by consumption or heavy spending
Draw in	– become shorter hours of day light; arrive at a station (for trains)
Draw into	– get involved in something unpleasant
Draw on	– pass slowly (time); inhale smoke from a cigarette, cigar, etc.
Draw out	– prolong something (usually far beyond the normal limits); make something continue longer than needed; make a shy person more outgoing
Draw up	– prepare a contract; write (contract, agreement, document); come to a stop (vehicles); organise
Dream of	– not think or consider
Dream up	– invent something; have an idea
Dredge up	– discover things about someone's past
Dress down	– dress casually; scold
Dress up	– dress very smartly; wear elegant clothes; disguise oneself
Drift apart	– slowly cease to be close to or friends with someone
Drift off	– start to fall asleep
Drill down	– search through layers of information on a computer

Drill down through – get to the bottom of something; get detailed data

Drill into – repeat something many times to make someone learn it

Drink up – finish a drink

Drive away – force an animal or someone to leave a place

Drive back – repulse; force back

Drive by – do something out of a car

Drive off – drive away from a place

Drive out – force someone to leave a place

Drive up – make something increase

Drone on – talk boringly for a long time

Drop around – visit someone, often without making an arrangement; deliver

Drop away – become smaller, in amount, numbers

Drop back – move back in a position/group

Drop by – pay a brief visit; visit informally (and usually without scheduling a specific time)

Drop in – to pay a short visit, often without information; visit informally; come without an appointment; visit, usually on the way somewhere

Drop off – deliver someone or something; fall asleep, to stop a vehicle and let someone get out; to take something (or someone) to a place and leave it there; to fall asleep (often unintentionally); decrease in number or amount

Drop out – stop attending/leave school or an organization; leave school without finishing; drop out of; quit a class, school, etc.

Drop over	– visit for a short time
Drop someone in it	– get someone into trouble
Drop through	– come to nothing; produce no results
Drown in	– cover excessively
Drown out	– be so loud that another sound cannot be heard
Drum into	– to make someone learn or believe something by constant repetition
Drum out	– force someone out of their job or position
Drum up	– increase support or interest
Duck out of	– avoid doing something
Duff up	– beat or hit someone repeatedly
Dumb down	– reduce the intellectual level of something in search of popularity
Dwell upon/Dwell on	– spend a lot of time on something; emphasize

□

E

Ease off – reduce pressure; become less severe or slow down (pain, traffic, work)

Eat away – destroy slowly

Eat in – eat at home

Eat into – use something valuable when you don't want to

Eat out – eat in a restaurant; dine in a restaurant; have a meal in a restaurant

Eat up – to eat all of something; to consume; to greatly disturb emotionally; consume something you don't want to consume

Ebb away – disappear gradually

Edge out – gradually push someone or something out of their position

Edge up – approach slowly

Egg on – encourage; urge/encourage greatly towards doing something (usually something negative)

Eke out – make something like money last as long as possible

Embark on/Embark upon – start a project or venture

Empty out – empty something completely; remove something or everything from a container

End in – finish in a certain way; result in

End up – arrive somewhere as a result or consequence; finally reach a state; place or action; eventually reach/do/decide; finish in a certain way; or place; finally arrive at; arrive at an unexpected place; do something unplanned

End up with – get as a result of something

Enlarge on – say more about something

Enter for – join or enter a competition

Enter into – become involved in or accept; begin; commence

Even out – eliminate differences of opinion; make something equal or level

Expand on – say more about

Eye up – look carefully at someone

□

F

Face off	– confront
Face up	– have courage to deal with, especially responsibilities; admit to, take responsibility for; relax; calm down
Face up to	– accept an unpleasant truth
Faff about/Faff around	– show amusement, especially laughing; behave indecisively; laugh a lot
Fall apart	– break into pieces; become emotionally disturbed and unable to behave normally; fall into pieces
Fall back	– retreat
Fall back on	– be able to use in an emergency; use as a last resort; retreat
Fall behind	– fail to keep up pace; make less progress
Fall down	– fall on the ground; have a weak point; become controlled; to be shown to be not true or good
Fall for	– be attracted to somebody; fall in love, believe a lie or a piece of deception; be deceived by; be in love with

Fall in – collapse; meet by chance; coincide with

Fall into – start doing something unplanned

Fall off – decrease; drop from

Fall out – argue and be on bad terms with someone (of hair, teeth), become loose and unattached, separate from an interior; to quarrel

Fall over – to stop working suddenly

Fall through – be unsuccessful; fail to come to completion; fail; miscarry; not happen; doesn't happen

Fall to – start an activity eagerly

Farm out – give or contract work to someone else

Fart about – waste time doing silly things

Fart around – waste time doing pointless things; to waste or spend time doing pointless or unnecessary things

Fasten down – tie something so that it doesn't move

Fasten on – give attention to something that confirms your beliefs

Fasten onto – follow someone closely, normally when they don't want your company; give attention to something that confirms your beliefs

Fasten up – close, attach

Fathom out – understand something

Fatten up – give an animal a lot to eat to make it fat

Fawn on/Fawn over – praise someone in an excessive way to get their favour or something from them

Fear for – worry

Feed off – eat a food as part of an animals diet; use something to your advantage

Feed on – grow stronger, consume in an animal's diet, give someone a particular food

Feed up – give someone a lot of food to restore their health; make them bigger, etc.

Feel up to – feel strong enough or comfortable enough to do something; touch sexually; grope; feel capable of doing something

Fend for – take care of yourself or someone with help from other people

Fend off – resist something successfully; push an attacker away

Ferret out – search and discover something

Fess up – confess; admit something reluctantly; give

Fess up to – confess, admit reluctantly to something

Fiddle around/Fiddle about – waste time doing silly things, or doing things unsuccessfully; make small movements with your hands

Fight back – defend yourself; resist an attack; try to control emotion and keep it hidden

Fight it out – struggle to see who wins, both by arguing or fighting

Fight off – fight an attacker and force him back; resist an illness or emotion

Fight out – decide

Figure on – plan; expect

Figure out – logically find the answer to a

problem, solve a problem by thinking about it carefully; understand why someone behaves the way she/he does

File away – put a document in the correct place for storage in a filing system

Fill in – add information to a form; to complete (a form); temporarily do someone else's work; temporarily substitute for another person; supply information that someone doesn't know; to write information in blanks

Fill in for – substitute

Fill in on – give someone information

Fill out – complete (a form/an application); become less thin; gain weight

Fill up – fill something completely; fill to the top; fill to capacity

Filter in – move into a lane of traffic without making other cars stop

Filter out – remove something unwanted

Find out – discover; discover or obtain information; learn/get information; to make an effort to discover or get to know (something)

Finish off – finish completely

Fink on – give away secrets about someone

Fink out – fail to keep a promise, arrangement, etc.

Fire away – ask questions

Fire off – send quickly, angrily (letter, emails, etc.); shoot/fire a gun (usually repeatedly)

Fire up – start a computer; excite; become excited

Firm up – make things clearer in a negotiation or discussion

Fish for – try to get some information or to get someone to say something

Fish out – remove something from a bag, pocket, etc.; remove from water, such as the sea, rivers, etc.

Fit in – get on in a group of people; have enough time or space for something

Fit into – become part of

Fit up – frame someone; make them look guilty of something they haven't done, provide equipment

Fix up – make an arrangement

Fizzle out – end in an unsuccessful way

Flag down – signal at a vehicle to get it to stop

Flag up – raise an issue, or highlight its importance

Flake out – fall asleep out of exhaustion

Flame out – fail

Flame up – burn brightly

Flare out – get angry suddenly

Flare up – when trouble suddenly appears

Flesh out – add more details or information

Flick over – change TV channels quickly

Flick through – change TV channels repeatedly; look through something quickly

Flip off – extend your middle finger as a gesture of contempt

Flip out – become very excited and lose control

Flip through – look quickly through a magazine, book, etc.

Flog off – sell something cheaply to get rid of it

Floor it	– drive a vehicle as fast as possible
Flounce off/Flounce out	– leave a place or walk away angrily
Fly about/Fly around	– circulate (rumours, etc.)
Fly at	– attack, criticise or shout angrily
Fly by	– when time appears to move quickly
Fly into	– change emotion quickly
Fob off	– make or persuade someone to accept something, lie or deceive someone
Fob off on/Fob off onto	– make or persuade someone to accept something you don't want
Fob off with	– make or persuade someone to accept something of lower quality than they want
Focus on	– concentrate on something
Fold up	– make a sheet of paper smaller
Follow on	– leave to meet someone after they have left the place you're at
Follow on from	– be the part of something
Follow through	– do what is necessary to complete something or make it successful
Follow up	– do something to check or improve an earlier action; find out about a problem and act; act upon a suggestion; take more action
Fool around	– not be serious; be unfaithful
Forge ahead	– make a lot of progress in a short time; move forward very quickly
Freak out	– become very disturbed or angry
Freeze out	– shut out or exclude by unfriendly treatment; force to retire or withdraw from membership, a job, etc.
Freeze over	– become covered with ice (lake, river, pond, etc.)

Freeze up – be blocked with ice, stop working because the parts of a machine won't move when a computer stops working; be paralysed with fear

Freshen up – wash quickly and improve appearance; add more alcohol to a glass before it is empty; quickly improve the appearance of something

Front for – represent someone, especially when covering illegal or wrongful activities

Front off – confront someone and let them know you are prepared to fight

Front onto – face (of a building)

Front out – face up to someone, withstand criticism

Front up – appear somewhere for a short time; advance cash for something

Frown on – disapprove of

☐

G

Gad about/Gad around	– visit a lot of different places for pleasure
Gag for	– want something a lot
Gang up	– form a group against something or someone
Gang up on	– harass bully
Gear up	– get ready for a busy period
Geek out	– talk at length about computing
Get	– pass (an exam) be connected on the phone
Get about	– visit many places, become known, walk or visit places have personal or sexual relationships with many people
Get above	– behave as if you are better or more important than others
Get across	– communicate successfully, go from one side to the other, move something from one side to the other, be convincing or make a good impression
Get across/over	– communicate, make understandable
Get after	– nag or exhort someone, chase

Get ahead of – move in front of

Get ahead/Get along in – progress

Get along – have a good relationship, leave, progess

Get along – have a friendly relationship (with), be friendly (toward), be on good terms, work well with, to have a good relationship with, to progress or handle, like each other

Get along with – have a good relationship with someone, deal with, handle

Get around – avoid having to do something; move from place to place; have mobility; do something eventually; persuade someone

Get around to – finally manage to do something; make the effort to do something

Get at – criticise; mean; be able to reach, find, access; use threats, payments, bribes, etc. to affect someone's testimony or decision

Get away – go on a vacation; to escape; do without being noticed or punished; to do something wrong or illegal without being punished (usually without even being discovered or caught)

Get away from – go somewhere different or do something different, start to talk about something that is not relevant to the discussion

Get away with – not get caught, criticised or punished for doing something wrong; achieve something, despite not doing it correctly or properly

Get back – receive something you had before, return; return something; revenge; move away

Get back at – retaliate; take revenge

Get back into – start doing something after stopping for some time; find a new enthusiasm for something

Get back into something – become interested in something again

Get back to – respond to a contact; respond when you know the answer; start doing something again after an interruption

Get back together – restart a relationship

Get behind – support

Get behind with – be late paying instalments for something

Get by – manage to cope or to survive, financially, in a difficult situation

Get by on – manage on a certain amount of money

Get by with – have enough of something to do the job

Get down – make someone depressed, unhappy, exhausted, etc.; write record; manage to swallow, descend; leave a vehicle; leave the table after eating; reduce

Get down on – criticise

Get down to – start working seriously, enjoy something a lot

Get in – arrive, enter, enter a small, closed vehicle

Get in on – become involved, become interested or excited, have sex

Get in with – become friendly with; ingratiate with

Get into – become involved or interested; become involved in something bad or criminal; be accepted or admitted; become or be accepted as a member; start a habit or way of acting or behaving; be small enough to wear something; criticise

Get it – be punished or scolded

Get it off with/Get it on with – have sex with

Get it together – control things in your life to achieve your aims; begin a relationship

Get it up – become aroused (of a man)

Get off – escape a punishment; be acquitted; go to sleep

Get off it – a way of expressing disbelief

Get off on – enjoy a drug; become excited by

Get off with – have casual sex with

Get on – make progress with a task; be successful in ones' life or caree; have a friendly relationship

Get on at – criticise unfairly

Get on for – approach a certain age/time/ number; be near a time

Get on to – start to suspect

Get on with – have a good relationship; continue or start doing something

Get onto – start discussing a topic; be elected, appointed; appear on the radio or TV, contact someone because you need or want them to do something; enter a plane, train, etc.

Get out – expression of disbelief; leave the house to visit a place and socialise; become known when people want it to remain secret; leave a place, escape; remove something from where it is stored to be used; remove dirt or something unwanted; publish; make available for the public to see or buy; say what you want when it is difficult

Get out of – avoid doing something you dislike; leave a car, van, etc.; stop a regular activity or habit; make someone confess or tell the truth; make someone give something to you; derive pleasure or benefit from something; help someone avoid doing something

Get over – recover from something; feel better; solve; find a solution; communicate; make people understand; be shocked or surprised that something if real or true; get to the other side; come somewhere

Get over with – do something unpleasant that has to be done rather than delaying it any more

Get rid of – dismiss someone, fire someone from a job; cause someone to leave; dispose of; give away or throw away; eliminate

Get round – to solve or avoid a problem, to persuade someone to do what you want; become known; find a solution

Get round to – find time to do

Get through – contact; consume; finish, succeed in an exam or test; help someone or something succeed or pass a test or exam; endure or deal with a difficult experience; be accepted or passed (laws, proposals, etc.); manage to pass, arrive, survive, finish

Get through to – make someone understand; contact, especially by phone; reach a stage in a competition

Get to – annoy; irritate; arrive; start discussing a topic; finish; to complete; reach

Get together – meet each other; meet socially

Get up – get out of bed; organise; leave bed after sleeping and begin your daily activities; rise; stand

Get up to – do something wrong or naughty; do something, usually bad when about children; colloquial

Get with – finish

Give away – betray, give something to someone else for free, entrust your daughter to her husband through the marriage ceremony; tell a secret, often unintentionally; distribute something for free; give without asking for or expecting payment; give an advantage to your opponent in a sport by making a mistake; playing badly; etc.; give an unwanted baby to people to bring up, betray; report to authorities; give a weight advantage to an opponent in boxing

Give back – return something you've borrowed; return something that someone has lost

Give in – stop doing something because it's too hard or requires too much energy; submit homework, etc.; surrender; accept defeat, offer or submit for judgement, approval

Give in to – agree to something you don't like; allow a feeling or desire to control you; criticise harshly or punish someone for something

Give it up for – applaud

Give of – contribute without expecting anything in return, usually time or money

Give off – emit pollution or something unpleasant; behave in a way that makes people think of you in a certain way; expand; follow or take one of two or more branches (instructions, in machine code) in writing a computer program (using system software for a programming language)

Give onto – open into a place, for a door or window

Give out – distribute, stop working, through age or overuse, have no more of a supply; make public; emit; end or finish somewhere; make a sound or noise; read the wordings of a hymn or psalm aloud for congregational singing

Give over – abandon; devote; stop; colloquial; an expression of disbelief; stop doing something bad or annoying; entrust; pass on responsibility; stop an activity

Give over to – dedicate; devote; transfer responsibility

Give something out – give to many people (usually at no cost)

Give up – stop doing something that has been a habit; stop being friendly; end relationships; surrender; stop trying; sacrifice or dedicate time, etc. to something; allow someone to sit in your chair; take your place, etc.; allow or give away a run while pitching

Give up on – lose faith in or stop believing in something or someone; stop feeling hope

Give up to – denounce; report to authorities

Give way – stop to allow vehicles to pass; collapse; break

Give way to – yield; surrender; retreat; relinquish position of ascendancy; be replaced by something better, cheaper, more modern, etc.; allow a vehicle to pass in front; surrender to strong emotions

Give yourself up – surrender to the police or authorities

Give yourself up to – dedicate time, energy, etc. to something

Gloss over – try to minimise the importance of something

Gnaw at – trouble; worry or annoy someone; harm gradually

Gnaw away at – harm gradually

Go about – deal with something; circulate

Go across – move to another side or place

Go after – chase; try to get

Go after someone – follow someone

Go after something – try to achieve something

Go against – be contrary to (principles, rules); oppose; lose a decision or a verdict of a court

Go against someone – compete; oppose

Go ahead – start; proceed

Go ahead with/Go on to – proceed

Go along with – accept a decision or suggestion; take the same view

Go around – circulate; be or have enough of something; visit

Go at – attack or approach something with vigour

Go away – depart; leave a place or disappear

Go back – have a long history; return to a place; start doing something again

Go back on – break a promise

Go before – precede

Go below – leave the top deck of a ship

Go by – the passing of time; trust or depend on for correct information; pay a short visit, call

Go down – decrease; get smaller, sink, sunset; be sent to a prison; become recorded as or known as, be eaten or swallowed, fall to the ground; happen, take place; stop working; especially computers; become dimmer; be received by people, in terms of their reaction

Go down on – perform oral sex

Go down to – be defeated

Go down with – fall ill; find acceptance

Go for – a person, an animal to attack, pick up; go and get; enter a competition, attack, be attracted to; choose; select; try to get; have something favourable; pass for or serve as

Go for it – be assertive and ready to initiate action

Go forth – leave a place; travel abroad

Go forward – move clocks ahead; progress

Go in – go to a hospital for treatment, surgery, etc.; fit; disappear; become obscured by a cloud; attack

Go in for – enter a competition or sit in an exam; support; advocate; like, have an interest in; make a career choice

Go in with – form a union or alliance; join; enter

Go into – discuss in some detail; enter a profession, hospital, trade, market; begin a speech or description; be dedicated or devoted; be contained in a larger number

Go it – behave in a reckless way; move or drive very fast

Go it alone – do something without help

Go off – explode (bomb); start ringing (alarm); go bad, start to dislike, leave a place, take place; follow a plan or pattern, stop working (electric/electronic equipment); to explode or fire (of alarms or alarm clocks); to ring suddenly; become bad (food) happen; continue

Go off with – elope; run away with someone; steal

Go on – continue; happen; start doing or taking something; be guided; be nearly a certain period of time; progress; spend money; start working (electric/electronic equipment)

Go on about – talk too much

Go on at – pester; try to make someone do something by repeatedly asking or suggesting

Go on with – continue doing

Go one – a way of encouraging someone

Go out – stop burning be extinguished leave a place; go on strike; become infashionable; move backwards (of a tide); be eliminated in a competition, be transmitted; be sent; intend

Go out for – become a candidate; apply for something

Go out to – feel sympathy with someone

Go out with – have a relationship with

Go out with someone – date

Go over – inspect the details of something; review; visit someone nearby, look at something; revise, visit, be approved or accepted; repeat or explain; clean

Go over to – go on a journey; become converted; change to something different

Go past – pass without stopping

Go round – be enough; visit informally; be or have enough of something; circulate; visit

Go through – experience; read again; examine; search; do something in a certain way or following certain procedures; explain; be approved formally or sanctioned; enter; consume or spend; perform or carry something out

Go through with – complete a promise or plan usually unwillingly; do or complete something you've agreed to

Go together – harmonize or be compatible

Go towards – contribute

Go under – go bankrupt; lose consciousness; sink

Go up – rise or climb; approach; be built; be heard, be promoted; increase in price; explode

Go up to – approach; attend a university; reach

Go with – combine nicely; accompany; accept; agree to; have a relationship with, look good with; to match or suit (something); look pleasing together (Note: for clothes, furniture, etc.)

Go without – not have, cope without having something

Goof around – fool around, not be serious

Goof off – avoid or leave work; be lazy; do nothing in particular

Goof up – mess; spoil

Grass on/Grass up – report someone to a person in authority

Grey out – disable a function in a computer program; leaving it visible but not working

Grind away – keep working at something

Grind down – reduce or destroy someone's enthusiasm

Grind into – press or twist something hard into something else

Grind on – proceed relentlessly; talk endlessly

Grind out – produce something with great difficulty

Grind up – reduce to small pieces

Grow apart – become distant; stop having a close relationship because time, distance, interests, etc. have changed

Grow away from – become less friendly with

Grow back – re-grow

Grow from – result from a process

Grow into – grow to fit large clothes; mature or change into; develop or change over time to fit something

Grow on – become more attractive; to become more liked; colloquial; like something that you didn't like at first, have a greater influence or degree of acceptance; become gradually more evident

Grow out – let hair, etc. with dyes; perms grow to get rid of the style

Grow out of – grow too large for clothes; lose interest as you grow older or become more mature; result or develop from

Grow to – eventually do something

Grow together – gradually become attached; united or close

Grow up – mature; become adult; arise, emerge; develop in a place or for a reason (city, town, etc.); spend one's childhood; behave responsibly

Grow up on – do or have something when you are a child

Grow upon – like something that you didn't like at first; have a greater influence or degree of acceptance; become gradually more evident

Guard against – take precautions

Gun for – try to destroy an opponent

□

H

Hack around	– waste time
Hack into	– break into a computer system
Hack off	– annoy
Ham up	– perform or act in an excessive way to attract attention or amuse people
Hammer away at	– work relentlessly
Hammer into	– repeat something over a period of time to make someone remember it
Hammer out	– negotiate and reach an agreement
Hand back	– return
Hand down	– pass on to the next generation; give a formal decision; give something used to someone else
Hand in	– submit work for appraisal; submit homework, an assignment, etc.
Hand on	– give to someone else; transmit knowledge to the next generation
Hand over	– give (usually unwillingly)
Hand something out	– to distribute to a group of people
Hang about	– spend time somewhere not doing much; stop what you're doing and pay attention to me

Hang around	– stay in a place
Hang back	– not move forwards to avoid doing something
Hang back from	– delay or avoid doing something
Hang in	– stay positive
Hang in there	– persevere; not give up
Hang on	– wait a short time (informal); grab; hold tightly
Hang onto	– keep; colloquial
Hang out	– spend time in a particular place or with a group of friends; spend time relaxing (informal)
Hang out for	– wait or refuse to do something until you get what you want
Hang over	– worry or trouble
Hang together	– work together when things are difficult
Hang up	– end a phone conversation; put something on hook or receiver
Hang up on	– end a phone call with someone
Hang with	– spend time with
Hanker after/Hanker for	– want something a lot, especially if you shouldn't want it or can't have it
Harp on	– talk repeatedly about something
Have against	– dislike, disagree or hold a grudge (usually negative)
Have around/round	– entertain someone in your home
Have down as	– think of someone or something in a particular way
Have in	– have a supply of something in a particular place; get someone to do some work; entertain people in your home
Have it away	– have sex with someone, especially casual sex

Have it in for – hold a grudge; be deliberately unkind to someone, also as have got

Have it off – have sex

Have it out with – discuss or argue an issue to improve a situation; express feelings so as to settle a problem

Have off – take time off work

Have on – be wearing; have an electronic device switched on; have an arrangement; tease; deceive; be in possession at a particular time; know something about someone that could harm them

Have over – receive a guest

Have someone on – try to make someone believe something that is untrue

Have to do with – be about

Have up – make someone appear in court

Head for – move or travel towards

Head off – stop someone or force them to change direction; prevent something bad happening; leave somewhere to go to another place

Head out – go out

Head up – be in charge

Hinge on – depend on

Hit at – aim a blow at

Hit back – retaliate; reply to an attack

Hit it off – get on well with

Hit on/upon – find unexpectedly or by inspiration; discover by chance, often an idea

Hold against – have a grudge against someone, or little respect

Hold back	– Hide an emotion; prevent something moving forwards or progressing; not disclose information or make it public
Hold back from	– not allow yourself to do something
Hold down	– keep a job; stop someone or something from moving
Hold forth	– state your opinions about something, especially when talking for a long time and boringly
Hold off	– when bad weather doesn't appear; stop someone from attacking or beating you
Hold on	– wait, grip tightly; wait a short time
Hold onto	– keep as long as possible; hold tightly; hold someone/something firmly using your hands or arms
Hold out	– resist; hold in front of you; offer, especially with hope
Hold out against	– try to reject
Hold out for	– wait for something better or refuse something now for something better in the future
Hold out on	– not pay someone or give them information
Hold over	– delay; to continue something for longer than planned
Hold someone/ something back	– prevent from doing/going
Hold someone/ something up	– rob
Hold together	– not break up
Hold up	– rob; threaten someone with harm if he/she does not give her/his

	money or other valuable things, use as an example, i.e. a model of good behaviour; to cause a delay, to rob someone, usually threatening violence; to stop; to delay; raise; lift to a higher than normal position
Hold with	– accept (usually negative), agree with an idea
Home in on	– target; focus
Hook up	– meet someone
Hook up to	– connect to a machine
Hoon around	– act in a dangerous or reckless way, especially when driving fast
Horse around	– not be serious
Hound out	– force someone out of a place, job, position, etc.
Hunker down	– settle in a place as comfortably as possible to stay there
Hunt down	– search for someone to punish or kill them
Hunt out	– search until you find something
Hunt up	– search for and manage to find something
Hurry up	– be quick; act speedily

□

I

Inquire into – investigate

Iron out – to remove small problems or irregularities from; resolve by discussion; eliminate differences; mutually reach an agreement; mutually resolve difficulties

Issue forth – come out of a place

□

J

Jack around – make trouble for someone; fail to keep promises

Jack in – quit; give up; abandon

Jack up – raise a car to be able to do mechanical work, increase sharply; raise (used for prices); raise/life by using a jack

Jam on – apply or operate something forcefully

Jaw away – talk just for the point of talking rather than having anything to say

Jazz up – make something more interesting or attractive

Join in – participate

Join up – engage in; become a member of; meet and unite with

Joke around – be funny; or try to

Jot down – make a quick note; take quick notes

Juice up – make something more exciting or perform better

Jump all over – severely scold someone; berate someone

Jump at – accept eagerly

Jump in – enter a conversation

Jump on – criticise, attack

□

K

Keel over – turn upside down; surrender; give in; fall to the ground

Keep around – keep something near you

Keep at – continue with something difficult

Keep away – prevent from/avoid being near; remain at a distance

Keep back – maintain a safe distance; withhold

Keep down – not vomit; not to increase

Keep from – control yourself; refrain; not tell

Keep in – not allow someone out

Keep off – not talk about; not tread on something; avoid (a topic); stay away

Keep on – continue doing something; continue to remind someone to do something until he/she does it (even if this irritates her/him); persevere

Keep out – not allow someone to enter

Keep someone/ something out – stop from entering

Keep something from someone – not tell

Keep something up – continue at the same rate

Keep to	– stay within limits; adhere to
Keep up	– not let someone go to bed; maintain a continuous action; persist; continue at the same rate, continue, carry on
Keep up at	– continue, not quit
Keep up with	– maintain pace with; not to fall behind somebody; stay at the same level as someone or something
Key in	– enter numbers or information into a computer or electronic system
Kick about/Kick around	– discuss
Kick around with	– spend time with
Kick back	– pay someone illegally as part of the price; resist
Kick down	– break something with your feet
Kick in	– to take effect (as in a drug); to break something by kicking it; to contribute money
Kick off	– begin; start a game of football; die; when trouble starts, argue, protest and refuse to co-operate
Kick out	– expel; force someone to leave because of his/her poor performance or unacceptable behaviour
Kick up	– cause trouble or pain
Kiss off	– used to tell someone to go away; consider something to be unimportant or inferior
Kiss up to	– try to get into someone's favour
Knock about	– beat someone
Knock around	– discuss casually
Knock back	– cost someone a lot of money;

finish a drink quickly; drink a lot of alcohol; shock

Knock down – demolish; hit and injure someone

Knock it off – stop doing something annoying

Knock off – finish work for the day; reduce the price of something; reduce the time required to do something; steal; produce or create something quickly

Knock oneself out – work much harder than normal or what is expected

Knock out – hit and make somebody unconscious; sell; distribute

Knock together – join houses that had been separate

Knock up – become or get someone pregnant; play a bit before a match to get ready; produce or create something quickly

Knuckle down – make a great effort

Knuckle under – submit to authority

□

L

Lap up – appreciate something

Large it up – have a good time when intoxicated

Lark about/Lark around – behave in a silly way

Lark it up – enjoy yourself noisily and exuberantly

Lash down – fall heavily (rain), secure something with ropes or cords

Lash into – criticise someone strongly

Lash out – suddenly become violent; react angrily, spend a lot of money on luxuries

Lash out against – criticise something strongly

Lash out at – hit someone suddenly, usually without warning, or try to hit them; criticise someone or shout at them

Lash out on – spend a lot of money buying something

Latch on – understand, often after a long time

Latch onto – connect to something; decide or realise that something is good or profitable

Laugh at – mock; make fun of

Laugh off – to pretend something serious isn't important; to pretend you are not bothered by something that really does bother you; ignore

Launch into – start; begin

Lay down – establish rules or procedures; kill; murder

Lay into – criticise angrily

Lay off – make an employee redundant, to stop employing (a worker), often for a short time because there is not enough work (not because of poor performance)

Lay on – organise; supply

Lay out – spend money

Lead to – result in

Leaf through – turn the pages

Leak out – become public

Lean on – put pressure on someone to get them to do what you want

Lean toward – prefer

Leave on – not turn off

Leave out – not include; omit; not mention; forget

Let down – fail to keep an arrangement; make clothes longer; fail to support or help; to disappoint someone (often by breaking a promise or an agreement)

Let in – allow someone to enter

Let in on – allow to be part of a secret

Let off – to excuse (someone) from a punishment, a duty, or doing something

Let on – inform about a secret

Let out – to allow (a person or an animal) to leave (a place); to release; make a sound; make clothes bigger

Let someone down – fail to support or help; disappoint

Let someone in – allow to enter

Let up – become less intense or slower

Lie down – rest

Lie with – have the right to make a decision

Lift off – leave the ground, rocket or spaceship

Light up – light or start smoking a cigarette; illuminate

Lighten up – be less serious

Limber up – do some exercises to warm up before playing a sport or other physical activity

Limber up for – prepare for something that will require a great effort

Line up – arrange in a line; arrange something in a line; arrange events for someone

Link up – connect; join

Link up with – connect with someone or contact them

Listen out for – listen for a particular noise or sound

Live by – follow a belief system to guide your behaviour

Live down – stop being embarrassed about something; suffer a loss of reputation

Live for – believe something is extremely important

Live in – live in the place where you work or study

Live it up – have a good time by spending a lot of money

Live off	– use money earned
Live on	– continue to live; use money for basic necessities; not be forgotten
Live out	– stay somewhere until you die; fulfil an ambition or fantasy; not live at the place where you study or work
Live through	– experience different times
Live together	– have a relationship and live in the same place without marrying
Live up to	– meet expectations or standards
Live with	– accept something unpleasant; have a relationship and live in the same place without marrying
Load down	– burden
Load up	– take illegal drugs; fill a machine or vehicle
Load up on	– consume a lot of something for a particular purpose
Lock away	– lock in a safe place; put someone in prison or a mental hospital for a very long time
Lock down	– make very secure
Lock in	– lock a place to stop someone leaving; commit someone in such a way that they cannot leave
Lock onto	– find a target and head for it
Lock out	– close a workplace to stop workers entering; lock a place to stop someone getting in
Lock up	– close all doors, windows, etc.; lock something in a safe place; put in prison or a mental hospital
Lock yourself away	– go somewhere away from people to study or work
Log in/on	– enter a restricted area on a computer system

Log off/out – exit a computer system

Look after – take care of; take care

Look after someone or something – to take care of someone or something

Look ahead – think of the future

Look back – think about the past

Look back on – to remember and think about the past; reflect on/consider something in the past

Look down – to think that someone (or something) is inferior, low or worthless; to disapprove of (someone or something)

Look down on – despise; hold in contempt; regard as inferior; regard with a feeling of superiority; have a low opinion of

Look for – try to find something; seek

Look forward – be excited about the future; anticipate pleasantly; to think with pleasure about a future event that you expect to enjoy

Look forward to – wait for or anticipate something pleasant

Look in – make a quick visit

Look in on – visit briefly to see if everything's all right

Look into – investigate/get more details about something; to carefully examine a situation or event and try to discover the reasons for it; investigate; research

Look like – resemble (in appearance)

Look on – be a spectator at an event; consider; watch something like a crime without helping

Look on as/Look upon as – consider; regard

Look out – be careful; vigilant; and take notice

Look out for – be especially vigilant for someone/something

Look over – check, examine, inspect hastily

Look round – inspect a house; to visit and tour round a place

Look something over – check; examine

Look something up – search and find information in a reference book or database

Look through – examine quickly; pretend not to see

Look to – expect; hope

Look up – consult a reference book; search and find information in a reference book or database; search in a list; to find (or try to find) something (e.g. a telephone number) in a book (e.g. a telephone directory); visit when in the area; find where someone lives or works and visit him/her

Look up to – have a lot of respect for; to admire (someone)

Look up to someone – have a lot of respect for

Lord it over – behave in a superior manner

Lose out – be at a disadvantage

Lose out on – not gain or have something advantageous

Lose out to – be less successful

Luck out – be unexpectedly lucky; be very lucky

□

M

Magic away	– make something disappear quickly
Make do with	– accept something less satisfactory because there's no alternative
Make for	– go to or toward; have/produce a particular effect; result in; cause, head in a certain direction
Make fun of	– laugh at/make jokes about
Make into	– change something into something else
Make it	– arrive or get a result
Make it up to	– try to compensate for doing something wrong
Make off	– run away
Make off with	– run away with; steal
Make out	– to make a check payable to; to pretend; to be able to see or hear something (a small detail or something in the distance); hear; understand; recognise; distinguish; to write (a cheque); progress; kiss and pet
Make over	– change appearance
Make someone out	– understand someone's behaviour

Make someone up – apply cosmetics to

Make something up – invent; lie about something

Make sure of – verify

Make up – invent (excuse, story); apply cosmetics to; compensate for something missed or not done by doing extra or equivalent work; constitute; form; invent a lie; put together; re-establish a friendly relationship by admitting guilt; to become friends again after a quarrel; stop being angry with someone; put on cosmetics; invent a story

Make up for – compensate

Make up to – increase a sum received to a higher figure

Make with – give (usually used as an imperative)

Mark down – give a student a lower grade for a particular reason; reduce the price of something; reduce the price (as an incentive to buy)

Mark down as – consider someone or something to be of a certain group, type, etc.

Mark off – tick; cross out or otherwise mark something to show that it has been dealt with

Mark out – delineate; draw lines to enclose an area

Mark out for – show promise for the future

Mark out from – stand out because of certain qualities

Mark up – increase the price (for resale); increase the price of something

Marry in – marry someone of the same ethnicity, religion, etc.

Marry out – marry someone of a different ethnicity, religion, etc.

Mash up – crush something until it becomes a paste; mix sources of audio; video or other computer sources; break or damage

Max out – take something to the limit; reach a limit

Mean to – intend

Measure against – evaluate or judge by comparison

Measure off – measure something and mark the point where it ends or will be cut

Measure out – measure or weigh the amount needed

Measure up – find the size of something; be good enough; meet the required standard

Meet with – have something happen to you

Mess about/Mess around – not be serious; not use something properly, treat someone badly

Mess around with – try to improve something, usually making things worse

Mess over – treat someone badly

Mess up – spoil or ruin; make something untidy or dirty; cause mental, physical or emotional problems

Mess with – become involved in something damaging or dangerous; annoy, bother, associate (negative); try to repair or improve; usually unsuccessfully

Mill around – walk around without going anywhere

Miss out – (lose a chance—colloquial); fail to include; not do something enjoyable or rewarding; not include

Miss out on – lose a chance; fail to achieve

Mistake for – to think wrongly that (one thing or person) is (another thing or person)

Mix something up – confuse two or more things

Mix up – confuse; make something lively; mistake one thing or person for another; cause to become confused

Monkey around – not be serious

Mooch about/Mooch around – spend time doing little or nothing

Mop up – resolve a problem; kill or capture the last few enemy soldiers after a victory; eat a sauce with bread to finish it; remove a liquid that has been spilt

Mope about/Mope around – move around being miserable

Mount up – increase over time

Mouth off – speak angrily about something

Move in – arrive in a new home or office

Move on – change the subject or your job; make people move from a place

Move out – leave your home/office for another one

Mug up on/Mug up – learn something quickly; revise

Mull over – think about an issue or problem

Muscle in – become involved in something when your involvement is not wanted

Muscle in on – become involved in something despite opposition to your involvement

Muscle into – become involved even though there is opposition to your involvement

Muscle out – use power, contacts, etc. to force someone out

□

N

Naff off – get lost; go away (used as imperative)

Nag at – repeatedly criticise someone verbally

Nail down – succeed in getting, achieve, understand fully; get full information from someone; succeed or achieve something

Name after – to give someone the same name as another person so as to honour or remember that person

Nip off/Nip out – go somewhere quickly

Nod off – fall asleep (usually unintentionally)

Nose about – look for something hidden or secret

Nose around – look around for evidence

Not care for – not like someone/something (formal)

Note down – write something; write something short like a phone number for future reference

Nut out – find an answer to a problem

☐

O

Occur to – enter one's mind

Open up – start to talk freely about something; open a shop or business for the day; allow goods into a market

Opt for – choose

Opt out – choose not to be part of something; leave a system or decide not to participate

Owe to – be the reason for something

Own up – to confess, admit or confess something, colloquial; to tell (someone) that you have done something wrong, or that you are at fault

□

P

Pack away – put something where it belongs

Pack in – stop doing something; end a relationship; fill a venue; breakdown; stop working

Pack it in – stop doing something (used as an imperative)

Pack off – send someone away

Pack out – fill a venue

Pack up – stop doing something; finish work; breakdown; stop working; collect things and put them where you keep them; stop an activity; to finish or stop doing something; to collect things and put them into a container for transporting; to bundle

Pad down – sleep somewhere for the night

Pad out – make a text longer by including extra content, often content that isn't particularly relevant

Pair off – begin a romantic relationship; introduce people, hoping they will start a relationship; form pairs

Pair off with	– form a pair with someone
Pair up	– form a pair
Palm off	– get someone to accept something that isn't true; pretend something is better than it is in order to sell it
Pan out	– succeed; happen as expected (for plans) (Note: almost always negative when in statements); the way a situation develops
Paper over	– try to conceal a problem without really fixing it
Pare back	– if you pare something back, you reduce the size or numbers
Pare down	– reduce; decrease
Part with	– give up reluctantly
Pass around	– give out to everybody there
Pass as	– be believed to be something
Pass away/Peg it	– die
Pass by	– go past without stopping; visit briefly; miss an opportunity
Pass for	– be accepted as something, usually when not
Pass off	– convince someone that something is real; happen in a certain way
Pass on	– give a message to someone; decline an invitation or opportunity; die
Pass out	– faint; lose consciousness
Pass over	– ignore someone and give a job, reward, etc., to someone who is junior
Pass something out	– give the same thing to many people
Pass something up	– decline (usually something good)
Pass through	– visit a place without stopping or only stopping briefly

Pass to	– give ownership or responsibility to someone
Pass up	– decline a chance
Patch up	– fix or make things better
Pay back	– reimburse; take revenge; repay money borrowed; take revenge on
Pay for	– purchase
Pay for something	– be punished for doing something bad
Pay into	– deposit money
Pay off	– completely repay a debt; produce a profitable or successful result
Pay someone back	– return owed money
Peck at	– eat very small amounts
Peg away	– keep working at something
Peg down	– fasten something to the ground
Peg out	– put washing outside to dry; die
Pencil in	– make a provisional appointment
Perk up	– feel better or happier; make someone feel better or happier
Peter out	– lose impetus and stop
Phase in	– introduce gradually
Phase out	– remove gradually
Pick at	– eat unwillingly; criticise
Pick off	– target individuals to change a group; eliminate
Pick on	– bother, annoy, criticise or make fun of someone; bully; intentionally try to make someone upset; be unkind to
Pick out	– choose; select; identify from a picture
Pick something out/ Plump for	– choose
Pick through	– search something that is disordered for something

Pick up – improve; learn quickly; collect; receive (a broadcast); collect (a person)—this differs from the 'collect a thing' meaning, as that means 'collect and bring back', whereas this means either (i) 'collect and drop off on your way' or (ii) 'collect and bring to the same destination'; arrange to meet someone and give her/him a ride; to collect someone or something (sometimes in a vehicle), collect somebody, get, buy, lift something off something else, take up, refresh, revitalize, improve

Pick up after – tidy a mess someone else has made

Pick up on – correct someone when they say something wrong; notice something that most people don't; react to something; comment on something said earlier in a conversation

Pick yourself up – recover from a fall or problem

Pig off – used to tell someone to get lost or leave you alone

Pig out – eat a lot

Pile up – accumulate

Pin down – get a fixed idea, opinion, etc. from someone; discover exact details about something

Pin on – attach the blame to someone

Pin someone down – force to give a clear statement, etc.

Pin up – fix something to a wall, or other vertical surface, with a pin

Pipe down – be quiet (often as an imperative)

Pipe up – to speak, raise your voice

Pit against – compete or force to compete

Pit out – go into the pits (car racing)

Pitch for – try to persuade someone to give your work, business, a job, etc.

Pitch in – help, join together to accomplish something; work together to help achieve an objective

Pitch into – criticise severely or attack someone

Play along – pretend; pretend to agree or accept something in order to keep someone happy or to get more information

Play around – be silly

Play at – pretend to be something; try

Play away – be sexually unfaithful when away from home

Play back – listen to or watch something you've recorded

Play down – try to make something seem less important

Play off – play a game to decide who the winner is; make people compete against each other so that you benefit

Play on – continue playing a sport though there might be a reason to stop; continue playing music; exploit a weakness; pun

Play out – progress, often till it finishes, pretend that something is real and reduce its effect; play something to the end

Play up – behave or work badly

Play up to – flatter someone

Play upon – exploit a weakness

Play with – touch and move something to occupy your hands; not eat much of a meal; consider something, but not seriously

Plead out – plead guilty to get a reduced sentence or fine

Plough back/Plow back – re-invest money you have made into a business

Plough into/Plow into – collide into at speed

Plough on/Plow on – continue doing something you don't want to

Plough through – eat a big meal; read something that is difficult or takes a lot of time; move through somewhere where there is little space or there are obstacles

Plough up/Plow up – break the surface of soil

Plug in – connect machines to the electricity supply

Point out – indicate/direct attention to something; call attention to; make someone aware of something; to draw attention to something or someone; indicate with your finger

Polish off – finish; consume

Polish up – improve something quickly

Pony up – pay for something

Poop out – get too tired to do something

Poop out on – fail to keep an appointment

Pop in – visit for a short time

Pop off – talk loudly; complain; go out for a short time

Pop out – go out for a short time

Pop up – appear, like windows and boxes opening on a computer screen, appear unexpectedly

Potter about/Potter around – spend time doing little things for pleasure

Pour down – rain heavily

Pour forth – emerge from a place in large numbers

Prattle on – talk too much

Press ahead/Press on – continue with something

Prey on – hunt and eat; disturb; procure

Price up – charge more for something

Print out – make a hard copy of a computer document

Prop up – support something, both physically and financially, politically, etc.

Provide for – prepare for

Psych out – work out or anticipate someone's intentions; make someone less confident

Psych up – prepare someone mentally

Pull ahead – overtake; move in front

Pull apart – destroy an argument, theory, etc.; stop people or animals fighting; make someone unhappy or upset

Pull away – when a vehicle moves from a place

Pull back – score a goal or point when losing; move away from a place, especially when talking about soldiers; move away from someone; decide not to do something or not to be involved with it any longer

Pull down – demolish; make someone depressed; earn

Pull for – support

Pull in – succeed in securing something earn a sum of money; arrest or take someone to a police station for questioning

Pull off – manage to do something difficult or tricky; start moving (vehicles); manage to succeed

Pull on – put clothes on

Pull out – start moving (train), move into traffic; withdraw; remove soldiers from an area

Pull over – stop by the side of the road; make a vehicle stop; drive a vehicle to the side of the road

Pull through – recover from and illness or problem

Pull to – close a door or window that has been left open

Pull together – work together as a team

Pull up – slow and stop a car, inform someone that they are wrong

Pull yourself together – become calm or regain control of your emotions

Push in – get in a queue without waiting

Push on – continue with some effort, colloquial

Put across – communicate ideas, express in an understandable way; communicate; convey a message

Put away – put something back in the correct place; put someone in prison; save or store

Put back – rearrange something for a later time; put something to its proper place; lay money aside for the future; move back the hands of a clock

Put by – save for the future

Put down – kill an animal because it's old, ill, etc.; stop holding (but withdraw support gently); repress; write down; store (food)

Put down for – commit to make a payment

Put down to – explain the cause of; give as a reason; attribute to

Put forward – move forward the hands of a clock; suggest; propose; to offer (a proposal/a plan, etc.) for consideration

Put in – install

Put in for – apply for a job; be a candidate for an election; make a request

Put off – to delay doing something until a late date; to delay an event or arrangement until a later date, to discourage or distract (someone) from doing; upset, postpone, arrange at a later date

Put on – turn on; switch on; begin to wear; don; to dress oneself; dress oneself with; tease; gain (weight); put clothing on the body; try to make someone believe something that is ridiculous or untrue

Put oneself out – take trouble, to help someone

Put out – broadcast, disturb or trouble someone; extinguish a cigarette, fire, etc.

Put somebody out – to cause inconvenience to someone

Put someone down – insult; make someone feel stupid;

put what you are holding on a surface or floor

Put through – connect someone by phone

Put together – assemble

Put towards – make a financial contribution

Put up – accommodate; give somebody a bed; build; raise (hand); provide accommodation for; offer for sale; return something to the proper place

Put up with – tolerate someone/something; to suffer (a difficult situation or person) without complaining

□

Q

Quarrel out – argue with someone about a specific subject

Quarrel with – dispute or disagree with something

Queer up – mess up; ruin

Quiet down – to become silent; fall silent

Quieten down – fall silent

Quit on – stop working, associating or being friends with someone, especially when they need support; stop working or functioning

□

R

Rack up – acquire a lot of something

Rain down on – fall in large numbers

Rake it in – make a lot of money

Rake up – bring something back to people's attention

Ramp up – increase price, speed or power of something

Rat on – inform authorities about someone's wrongdoings; fail to keep a promise

Rat out – inform the authorities about someone

Rat through – look for something hurriedly

Ratchet up – increase

Rattle off – to quote information quickly off the top of one's head

Reach out – stretch your arm to get something

Reach out for – try to achieve something difficult

Reach out to – ask for help; offer help; try to communicate and establish good relations with people

Read back – review

Read off – read a list aloud for someone to write down

Read out – read aloud rather than silently

Read over/Read through – peruse

Read up on – research

Reason with – try to persuade

Reckon on – calculate on the minimum expected

Reel in – catch a fish on a line and pull the line to land attract people, especially customers, to get them to do what you want them to

Reel off – quote statistics or facts rapidly; score a lot of points or win a lot of games one after the other

Reel out – unwind

Rein in – control someone or something to stop them causing more trouble

Rely on – count on; depend on; trust

Ride off – go away on a bike, horse, etc.

Ride on – depend on

Ride out – survive a difficult time

Ride up – move higher on the body (of clothes)

Ring back – return a phone call

Ring off – finish a phone conversation

Ring up – to make a telephone call

Rip off – charge excessively or obtain money unfairly; cheat; take advantage of; charge too much

Rise above – be superior to

Roll back – reduce; retreat; reduce or remove

Roll in – arrive somewhere, especially if late; arrive in large numbers for military vehicles

Roll on – when something continues to happen, said when you can't wait for something nice in the future

Roll out – introduce, launch or introduce a new product, initiative, etc.

Roll over – acquiesce

Roll up – an imperative used to attract people to a public event; to appear in large numbers for an event

Romp in – win easily

Romp through – do something easily or quickly

Room in – to keep a mother and baby together after the birth

Root about/Root around – look in a place to try to find something

Root for – support

Root out – look for and find, find the source of a problem and remove it

Root up – dig a plant out of the ground

Rope in – get somebody to help

Rough up – assault

Round off – change from a fraction to the nearest whole number; finish something in a satisfactory manner

Row back – retreat from a position

Rub along – have a reasonably good relationship

Rub down – dry or clean something with a cloth; massage or rub someone to help them relax

Rub in – apply a substance like cream or ointment and rub it until it is absorbed

Rub it in – emphasize how bad a situation is to make someone feel worse

Rub off on – pass a quality or characteristic to people

Rub out – delete ink or pencil with an eraser; kill

Rub up against – touch someone in a sensual or sexual way

Rub up on – revise

Rule out – eliminate; exclude a possibility

Run across – meet or find someone accidentally

Run after – chase; pursue; try to become romantically involved with someone

Run against – oppose; make difficulties

Run along – go away; leave (often as an imperative)

Run away – escape from a place or suddenly leave, flee; leave unexpectedly

Run down – hit a pedestrian with a vehicle; lose energy or power; criticise; disparage; find the source or origin of something, knock down; collide with; feel weak due to overwork; lose power; allow to decline

Run for – campaign for a position

Run in – arrest; take to police station for questioning; to use a new (or reconditioned) engine carefully until it is ready for normal use

Run into – cost; meet by accident

Run off – make photocopies; escape; flee

Run on – be powered by

Run out – have none left; run outside; become used up

Run out of – have no more of something; exhaust one's stock; exhaust supply

Run over – check; also run through; injured by a vehicle, overflow; study quickly; pass over; knock down someone/something; drive a vehicle over a person or thing, hit

Run over/through – rehearse; review; something

Run through – practise a dramatic work like a play quickly; stab or wound deeply with a knife, sword, etc.

Run to – go to someone for help; include in things you like; have enough money to buy something, often negative

Run up – move quickly to where someone is; hoist, raise a flag; do or make something very quickly; spend a lot of money on credit

Run up against – encounter problems, often unexpected

Run up on – approach someone without their knowing

Run with – keep company, normally bad

Rush into – do something too quickly

□

S

Sag off	– not go to school or work; leave early when you shouldn't
Sail into	– criticise angrily
Sail through	– pass easily; succeed
Sally forth/Sally out	– leave somewhere safe or comfortable
Salt away	– save money
Save on	– reduce or avoid consumption to cut costs
Save up	– for money for a particular purpose; collect or store something for future use; accrue
Scare away	– frighten someone so much that they go away
Scare off	– make someone so frightened that they go away
Scout about/Scout around/round	– look in different places for something
Scout out	– search for something
Scout up	– try to find someone for a task or requirement
Scrape along	– manage with little money
Scrape by	– to just barely manage to accomplish something

Scrape in – just get enough to succeed, pass or be accepted

Scrape into – be accepted somewhere, but only just

Scrape through – pass a test but only just

Scrape together/ Scrape up – manage to collect enough of something you need, usually money

Screen off – separate a part of a room with something like a curtain, screen, etc.

Screen out – exclude; block light; stop noticing something

Screw around – waste time; be sexually promiscuous

Screw up – do badly or fail

See about – arrange; consider

See into – accompany someone into an office

See off – chase somebody or something away; go to the airport, station, etc. to say goodbye to someone

See out – accompany a guest to your front door when they are leaving your house

See through – continue with something to the end; realise someone is lying or being deceitful

See to – deal with something

Seek out – pursue

Sell off – sell a business or part of it; sell something cheaply because you need the money or don't need it

Sell on – convince someone; buy something then sell it to someone else

Sell out	– have no more of something left because it has been bought; lose all artistic integrity in return for commercial success
Sell up	– sell a house or business to move somewhere or do something different
Send back	– return something
Send for	– ask someone to come and help
Send in	– order people into a place to handle a problem; write to get information
Send off	– expel a sports player from a match; post a letter
Send off for	– order something by post
Send out	– send something to a lot of people
Send out for	– order takeaway food by phone
Send something back	– return (usually by mail)
Send up	– imitate/impersonate for comic effect
Set about	– start doing something
Set aside	– overturn a court verdict or decision; reserve for later use
Set back	– cost; cause a delay in scheduling; hinder; slow down a progress
Set down	– write down
Set forth	– state or outline an opinion; start a journey
Set in	– change season noticeably
Set off	– explode a bomb; ring an alarm; start a journey; counterbalance a debt
Set on/set (up) on	– attack
Set out	– display; show; start a journey; arrange; give in detail in writing
Set someone up	– trick; trap

Set something up – arrange; organize
Set up – start a business; make arrangements for something; establish; to arrange; begin
Settle down – start living a fixed and routine life
Settle for – accept whatever is available; reluctantly accept
Settle in – get used to
Settle on – agree
Settle up – pay a debt
Sex up – change information to make it more attractive to the reader or listener
Shack up – live with someone when you are in a relationship; live somewhere temporarily
Shake down – search; extort or cheat money from someone
Shake off – get rid of an illness; rally
Shape up – develop in a positive way; improve to reach an acceptable standard
Shave off – shave completely, reduce by a small amount
Shell out – spend money on something, especially when you think it's too expensive
Ship – send goods to a place
Ship off – send someone away, often because of a problem
Ship out – leave a place
Shoot away – leave somewhere quickly
Shoot back – return quickly
Shoot off – leave promptly and quickly
Shoot out – go out for a short time
Shoot up – increase quickly; take illicit drugs

intravenously; damage with gunshots; increase quickly; grow

Shop around – look around for the best price, quality, etc.

Short out – short circuit

Show around/round – take someone to a place to show them certain parts

Show in – take someone into an office or other room

Show off – behave in a way so as to attract attention; display something you are proud of; make the qualities of another thing more apparent

Show out – take someone to out of a room or building

Show over – take someone around a site

Show through – when a feeling can be seen despite attempts to conceal it

Show up – appear/arrive; do a noticeably better job (often unexpectedly) than someone else; attend something or arrive somewhere; become clear or apparent; make someone feel embarrassed or ashamed

Shrug off – disregard something; not consider it important or harmful

Shut away – imprison or remove someone's freedom

Shut down – close a business, shop, etc.; turn a computer off

Shut in – prevent someone from leaving

Shut off – close; prevent access

Shut out – exclude

Shut out of – exclude someone from an activity, etc.

Shut up – stop talking or making noise; close for a period of time

Shut up (impolite) – be silent; stop talking

Shut yourself away – withdraw from company

Shy away from – avoid doing something because you lack confidence

Side with – support in a dispute; support someone

Sift through – examine a lot of things carefully

Sign away – give away legal or property rights

Sign for – write a signature on behalf of someone

Sign in – register in a hotel; open a computer program that requires a name and password; write your name when entering a place

Sign into – open a particular computer program that requires a name and password

Sign off – end a message, close a claim for unemployment benefit; stop doing something to leave; give someone a letter to be away from work

Sign on – open a claim for unemployment benefit; agree to participate; start broadcasting, employ

Sign on with – sign a document joining or agreeing to something

Sign out – close a computer program that requires a name and password; sign something to show you have borrowed something

Sign out of – close a particular computer program that requires a name and password

Sign up – give your name to do something; subscribe

Sign with – make a contract with

Simmer down – become calmer; make less noise

Sink in – realise slowly, colloquial, intransitive; slowly come to be understood

Sit about – sit and do nothing, especially when you should be working

Sit around – sit idly; doing nothing

Sit back – wait for something to happen without making any effort; relax in a chair

Sit by – not try to stop something

Sit down – help someone to sit; take a seat

Sit for – pose for an artist or photographer; look after children while their parents are out

Sit in – occupy a building to protest about something

Sit in for – take on someone's responsibilities while they are absent

Sit in on – attend as an observer

Sit on – be on a committee; to handle somebody firmly who behaves impertinently; conceitedly hold information back or keep it secret

Sit out – not take part

Sit over – eat or drink slowly

Sit through – stay till the end of something dull; sit and endure

Sit with – reconcile different positions

Size up – assess a situation or person carefully; make something bigger or produce bigger products

Skip out – desert

Skive off	– avoid doing work or other duty
Slack off	– reduce one's effort; perform with less enthusiasm and energy
Slag off	– criticise heavily
Sleep off	– lose; sleep in order to recover from excess alcohol, drugs, etc.
Sleep on	– think about something
Sleep over	– spend the night at someone else's house; stay somewhere for the night (informal)
Sleep through	– not wake-up
Slip out	– leave discreetly
Slip up	– make a mistake (colloquial)
Slob out/around	– be lazy; do nothing
Slope off	– leave somewhere without letting others know
Slough off	– get rid of; dispose; lose or shed outer layers of skin
Slow down	– reduce speed; become less active
Slow up	– slow the progress of something
Smack of	– appear to have a negative quality
Smash down	– demolish or break something down
Smash in	– break something by hitting it repeatedly
Smash up	– destroy; break into many pieces
Snap off	– break a piece off something
Snap out of	– control negative emotions
Snap to it	– do something quickly
Snap up	– get, acquire or buy something quickly
Sneak out	– abscond
Sneak up	– creep
Sniff around	– look around to see how good something is or to try to find something better

Sniff at – disapprove or be scornful

Sniff out – find something by smell (usually for dogs); find out information, especially when people don't want anyone to know

Soak up – to absorb; to become filled with (something)

Sober up – stop showing the effects of alcohol or drugs

Soldier on – continue even when things get difficult

Sort out – find a solution; resolve a problem

Sort something out – organize; resolve a problem

Sound off – to express your opinions forcefully

Sound out – check what someone thinks about an issue, idea, etc.

Spark off – cause something, usually unpleasant, to happen

Spark up – to begin a conversation, an argument, a friendship

Speak out – talk openly and freely

Speak up – talk more loudly; to speak louder

Spell out – explain something in full detail

Spew out – expel, throw out

Spew up – vomit

Spin off – produce an unexpected additional benefit; form a separate company from part of an existing one; create a TV show using characters from a popular show

Spin out – lose control (vehicle); make something last as long as possible

Spit it out – an informal way of telling someone to say something they are unwilling to say

Spit out – say something angrily

Split up – divide into groups; finish a relationship

Spoil for – really want something

Spur on – encourage someone to continue

Square away – finish or sort something out

Square off/ Square off against – confront someone or prepare to fight them

Square up – pay back a debt; confront someone or prepare to fight them

Square up to – accept responsibility or guilt

Square with – match; conform to; check with someone that something is OK

Squeeze up – get more people into a space than normal or comfortable

Stack up – put things in a pile; accumulate; increase; accumulate something; be logical; make sense; build-up the number of planes waiting to land at an airport

Stack up against – be as good as something

Staff up – employ someone for something specific

Stamp out – get rid of something

Stand about/Stand around – spend time in a place waiting or doing nothing or very little

Stand aside – leave a position so that someone else can take it

Stand back – keep a distance from something, try to understand something by taking a different perspective

Stand by – support someone; be ready and waiting for something to happen; keep to an agreement

Stand down – leave a job or position so that someone else can take it; finish being asked questions in a court

Stand for – tolerate; permit (usually negative), to represent or mean; to be a sign or short form of something else; initials

Stand in for – substitute someone temporarily; take the place of

Stand out – be extraordinary and different; be noticeably better than other similar people or things

Stand up – make a date but not keep it; rise to a standing position; move from a sitting or lying down to a vertical position; fail to keep an appointment

Stand up for – defend; support

Stand up to – keep your principles when challenged by an authority; resist damage; resist; bear stress

Start off – make something start; begin life; a career or existence; begin a journey; make someone laugh

Start off on – help someone to start a work or activity

Start on – begin to use or consume; criticise angrily

Start on at – criticise or nag

Start out – begin a journey

Start out as – begin life, existence or a career

Start out to – intend; plan

Start over – begin something again

Start up – open a business; begin, especially sounds, when an engine starts working, make an engine work; sit or stand upright because someone has surprised you

Stash away – store or hide something in a safe place

Stay away – not come
Stay away from – avoid; not come
Stay in – not go out
Stay on – remain longer than anticipated
Stay out – not go home
Stay over – stay overnight
Stay up – not go to bed
Steal away – leave
Steer clear of – avoid
Stem from – originate; be caused by
Step aside/Step down – leave a job or position so that someone else can take over
Step back – look at something from a different perspective
Step forward – offer help
Step in – get involved by interrupting something
Step on it – an imperative used to tell someone to go faster, especially when driving
Step out – leave a place for a very short time
Step to – confront; chat; talk to
Step up – increase
Stick around – stay in a place for some time
Stick at – continue doing something despite difficulties
Stick by – support someone when they are having difficulties; support a plan, opinion or decision
Stick down – write something quickly or without thinking about it; join surfaces with glue
Stick it to – criticise someone; treat someone badly or unfairly
Stick out – be easily noticed; extend part of your body; continue doing something difficult or unpleasant

Stick out for	– demand a salary raise
Stick to	– not change, restrict or limit and not change; adhere to something; continue doing something; limit yourself to one particular thing
Stick together	– support each other
Stick up	– stand on end; rob using weapons
Stick up for	– support or defend, especially yourself, your rights, colloquial
Stick with	– not change something; stay near someone; not be forgotten, continue with something difficult or unpleasant
Stir up	– make trouble for someone else
Stitch up	– sew something so that it is closed; finalise a deal; cheat someone or make them look guilty when they aren't
Stop around	– visit someone for a short time
Stop back	– return somewhere
Stop behind	– stay somewhere when other people leave
Stop by	– visit somewhere briefly or quickly
Stop in	– stay at home; visit briefly
Stop off	– break a journey
Stop out	– be out late, especially when you are expected home
Stop over	– stay somewhere when on a journey
Stop up	– stay up late; fill or block something
Storm off Storm out	– leave a place angrily
Stow away	– hide in a vehicle to travel without people knowing; store something in a safe place
Straighten out	– make something straight; deal

with a problem; make clear and resolve; improve someone's behaviour

Straighten up – stand straight, tidy

Strike back – attack; take action against someone who has hurt you

Strike down – kill; make someone ill; disallow a law, decision; reject, etc.

Strike off – remove someone's professional licence to practise

Strike on/Strike upon – have a good idea

Strike out – start doing something new and different; try to hit someone; start going towards a place; cross writing out

Strike up – start (conversation, relationship); start performing music; begin

String along – deceive someone for a long time; accompany someone because you haven't got anything better to do

String out – make something last as long as possible

String together – put words together into a coherent text

String up – hang somebody

Stub out – extinguish a cigarette

Stuff up – make a mistake; do badly; spoil

Stumble across – find accidentally, find something accidentally

Stumble upon – find something accidentally

Stump up – pay for something

Suck in/Suck into – become involved in something unpleasant

Suck up to – ingratiate yourself with someone

Sum up – summarise

Summon up – get the energy or courage to do something

Survive on – survive using

Suss out – come to understand

Swan about/Swan around – move in a dramatic or affected manner

Swan in – enter in a dramatic or attention-seeking manner

Swan off – leave somewhere in a defiant or pompous manner

Swear by – have great confidence in

Swear down – promise that something is true

Sweep through – pass easily; succeed; move quickly through

Swing around – change your opinion quickly; turn around quickly

Swing at – try to hit

Swing by – visit a person or place on your way somewhere

Switch something off – stop the energy flow; turn off

Switch something on – start the energy flow; turn on

Syphon off – take business, support or votes from someone; divert money illegally

□

T

Tack onto/Tack on – add or attach something that wasn't planned to something

Tag along – to go with someone, especially when you weren't invited; accompany someone, especially if they haven't specifically invited you

Tag onto/Tag on – add an additional point to something written or spoken

Tag with – add a keyword link or bookmark to a blog entry or webpage

Tail away – become silent or inaudible

Tail back – form a traffic jam

Tail off – become silent or inaudible; decrease

Take (it) out on – make someone else suffer because of one's own sufferings

Take after – look like; resemble, in appearance or character; follow as an example

Take apart – take something to pieces

Take aside – get someone alone to talk to them

Take away – remove

Take back – make someone nostalgic; retract a statement; admit that something was wrong; return an item

Take care of – make arrangements (for something to happen); take responsibility for; provide care for; watch one's health; look after; make a written note

Take down – make notes or write down in full; remove; to record in writing

Take in – to deceive (someone); to cheat (someone); understand (meaning); make clothes smaller

Take it – accept criticism

Take it out on – abuse someone because you're angry

Take it upon yourself – take responsibility, often without consulting other people

Take off – leave the ground; to rise from the ground; imitate, colloquial; leave; depart (often suddenly or quickly), make arrangements to be absent from work; remove (something you're wearing); start to fly

Take on – allow passengers on a ship or plane; assume a responsibility; employ

Take out – borrow a library book; borrow money from a bank or other official lender; extract or remove; go out socially with someone, especially a date, obtain insurance; kill; murder

Take over – gain control of; to assume responsibility for, or control of, (something or a situation) from someone else

Take to – develop a habit; develop a liking for

Take up	– fill or occupy time or space; make clothes shorter; start a new hobby, pastime, etc.
Take up time	– occupy time; to begin to study; practice or do (something)
Take up with	– begin to associate with
Take/bring back	– return
Talk back	– respond rudely to a person in authority
Talk back to	– answer impolitely
Talk down	– counsel; try to make something sound less important
Talk down to	– patronize; talk in a way to show your superiority
Talk into	– persuade someone to do something
Talk out of	– convince; persuade someone not to do something
Talk out of or into	– dissuade from; persuade into
Talk over	– discuss
Talk through	– explain; guide someone through an issue
Talk up	– make something appear more important or significant than it really is
Tall through	– to fail to happen or be completed (of plans, arrangements, schemes, etc.)
Tamper with	– interfere with
Tap for	– get money off someone
Tap into	– use or exploit a plentiful resource for your benefit
Tap off with	– have sex with
Tap out	– play a rhythm quietly
Tap up	– approach a footballer illegally to get them to change teams

Tear apart – disturb or upset greatly

Tear at – pull or try to pull something to pieces

Tear away – stop someone doing something unwillingly; remove a surface violently

Tear down – demolish

Tear into – criticise strongly or angrily

Tear off – remove part of a form or letter using your hands, not scissors; leave at high speed; remove with force

Tear up – Rip into pieces; destroy completely by tearing

Tee off – start or launch an event; place a golfball on a short plastic or wooden stick before hitting it at the start of a hole; annoy someone

Tee off on – criticise

Tee up – place a golfball on a short plastic or wooden stick before hitting it at the start of a hole; make preparations before starting or launching something

Tell apart – see a difference between two things

Tell off – chide; talk angrily to someone about something they've done wrong; speak to someone bluntly and negatively; saying exactly what she/he did wrong, to speak angrily to someone who has done something wrong; to find fault with someone

Tell on – report someone to an authority

Think back – remember (often + to, sometimes + on)

Think back on – recall
Think over – consider (something) carefully
Think through – consider all the possibilities and outcomes of a situation
Think up – create or invent something, especially when lying
Throw away – discard something when no longer needed; put in the garbage; forcibly make someone leave (usually because of bad behaviour); dispose of
Throw out – Get rid of
Throw up – vomit
Tick away/Tick by – pass (of time)
Tick off – annoy; scold; put a mark on an item in a list when it has been dealt with; irritate someone, make someone upset or angry, show that something has been completed by putting a tick (check) beside it
Tick over – continue working, but without improving; operate but without moving (engines); use something carefully so as not to finish it
Tidy up – put things in the correct place in a room
Tie back – fasten or secure so that it doesn't obstruct
Tie down – secure something to prevent it moving; remove or restrict freedom; stop people (often police or military) going where they are needed
Tie in – agree, be connected or support
Tie in with – occur at the same time, be in agreement with

Tie into – attack

Tie up – tie or fasten something securely; stop someone doing something; fasten; block a road, etc.

Tighten up – make something more secure or function better

Tip off – secretly inform the police or authorities

Tip over – spill; make something fall on its side

Tire of – get bored of something

Tire out – make someone exhausted to improve your knowledge, skill, or memory of (something you used to know, or do, but have now partly forgotten)

Toddle off – leave; go home

Tone down – make something sound more moderate

Tool up – provide equipment; arm yourself or somebody

Top off – finish something in a special way

Top out – stop increasing; reach the highest point

Top up – refill something that isn't empty yet

Touch down – land (planes)

Touch for – borrow money

Touch off – cause a problem to occur

Touch up – improve the appearance of something; touch someone in a sexual way

Touch upon/Touch on – mention

Toy at – pretend to think about or think about in a casual way

Toy over – think about something

Toy with – not eat much of a meal; consider something, but not very seriously; move or play with something to occupy your hands

Track down – find after a long search; trace the whereabouts of

Trade down – sell something and replace it with something cheaper

Trade in – exchange something old as part of the price of something new; leave your wife or husband to marry someone younger

Trade off – bargain; make a deal or compromise; accept something you don't really want to get something you do want

Trade on – exploit; use something to your advantage

Trade up – buy larger or more expensive items; leave your wife or husband and marry someone better looking, richer, etc.

Trade upon – exploit; use to your advantage

Trickle down – pass benefits from economic expansion through the economy to the less fortunate

Trip over – fall; fall because you hit an obstacle

Trip up – make a mistake

Trot out – make a statement (meant negatively)

Trump up – charge or accuse someone falsely

Try back – phone back

Try for – seek; make an attempt to get something

Try it on – provoke someone by being

annoying or behaving badly; attempt to get something, usually by deceit, without great hopes of success

Try on – wear something to see if it suits or fits; put clothing on to see if it fits, appraise; test a machine; use a machine briefly to determine how well it works; try to win a place in a team or other organization

Try out – test; test something to see if you like it or want to buy it

Try out for – be tested for a sports team

Try something on – sample clothing

Try something out – test

Tuck away – put something in a safe place; eat a lot

Tuck in – tidy the ends of items of clothing by placing them inside something; start eating enthusiastically; arrange the sheets, duvet or blankets to make someone, usually a child, comfortable in bed

Tuck into – start eating something

Tuck up – arrange the sheets, duvet or blankets to make someone, usually a child, comfortable in bed

Tune in/Tune into – watch or listen to a TV or radio programme

Tune out – ignore; not pay attention

Tune up – improve the performance of a machine or engine; tune a musical instrument before playing

Turn against – stop liking and start disliking

Turn around – make changes so that something that was unprofitable is profitable; move so that someone/something is facing the opposite direction

Turn away – not allow someone to enter a place

Turn down – refuse; decrease the volume; diminish the intensity; reject; lower volume; to refuse or reject (something or someone)

Turn in – give/deliver/submit to someone; go to bed; hand in report or deliver wrongdoers to the authorities

Turn into – to change; to become

Turn off – repulse; bore; repel (very informal); stop by turning a handle or switch; switch off, interest very much; excite (very informal); start by turning a handle or switch

Turn on – cause someone to feel attraction or pleasure; start a machine; attack

Turn out – produce; produce an unexpected result; stop a light; attend, switch off come to a meeting or to form a crowd; happen to be in the end

Turn over – give to the authorities; bring the reverse side up

Turn to – try to get help; take up a habit

Turn up – increase the volume or strength (heat, light etc.); appear suddenly; be discovered by chance; increase the intensity; make an appearance

Type up – type a finished version

□

U

Urge on – encourage; persuade or pressure to accept something

Urge upon – persuade or pressurise to accept something

Use up – finish the supply; to finish or consume all of something; finish a product (so that there's none left)

□

V

Vacuum up – consume

Veg out – relax; do nothing

Venture forth – leave somewhere safe or comfortable

Verge on – approach

Vouch for – express confidence in, or guarantee something

□

W

Wade through	– slowly peruse
Wait for	– wait until someone/something arrives or is finished with something else
Wait on	– serve (usually customers in a restaurant, shop, etc.)
Wake up	– rouse someone; cause someone to stop sleeping; stop sleeping
Walk off with	– steal
Walk out on	– abandon
Walk through	– demonstrate
Wallow in	– indulge
Wander off	– meander
Warm someone/ something up	– increase the temperature
Warm up	– prepare body for exercise
Watch out	– be careful
Watch out for	– be careful of; beware of
Watch over	– guard
Water down	– to make something weaker or less offensive
Wear off	– fade away; loose effect, especially a drug; to disappear gradually
Wear out	– cause to become exhausted; cause

to become very tired; to use (something) until it becomes unfit for further use; to become unusable after excessive use

Wipe off – clean (board, table)

Work off – eliminate

Work out – do physical exercise; find a solution or calculate something; exercise (usually in a gym, etc.) to build muscles, body tone, etc.; solve a problem/resolve a difficult situation (usually by working together); to produce a way of dealing with a problem or situation by thinking; be successful; calculate; work out for a specific amount; to solve a problem by calculation or study

Work something out – make a calculation

Work toward – pursue

Wrap up – finish something, bring something to a conclusion, wear enough clothes to keep warm

Write down – record something in writing

Write up – record, report in writing

□

Y

Yack on/Yammer on	– talk continuously, especially if it is an annoying way
Yammer on about	– to talk in an annoying way about something or complain about ("on" can be repeated for emphasis)
Yield to	– surrender

□

Z

Zero in on – direct or focus attention on; head for, move towards; if you zero in on something, you focus on it or put your attention on it

Zero out – cut off funding for a project; reduce to zero; cancel; remove

Zip around – if you zip around, you move quickly from place to place; move quickly

Zip by – pass quickly

Zip up – keep quiet; to do up a zipper in a piece of clothing or in a bag

Zone in/Zone in on – pay attention after not doing so

Zone out – if someone zones out, they look blankly ahead without paying attention, maybe because they're tired or bored or affected by drugs; to not pay attention; allowing your mind to go blank; dissociate yourself from a situation

Zonk out – fall asleep; fall asleep quickly because of exhaustion

Zonked out – if you're zonked out, you're very

tired and you feel like resting or going to sleep

Zoom in – focus more closely, if a photographer or a camera zooms in, the image changes so that it looks as if the camera is moving closer to the object being photographed or filmed

Zoom in on – focus more closely

Zoom off – go somewhere quickly

Zoom out – focus less closely

□□□